Who Works Here?

Hospital

by Lola M. Schaefer

Heinemann Library
Chicago, Illinois

© 2000 Reed Educational & Professional Publishing
Published by Heinemann Library,
an imprint of Reed Educational & Professional Publishing,
100 N. LaSalle, Suite 1010
Chicago, IL 60602
Customer Service 888-454-2279

Printed in Hong Kong
Designed by Made in Chicago Design Associates

04 03 02 01 00
10 9 8 7 6 5 4 3 2 1

Library of Congress Cataloging-in-Publication Data

Schaefer, Lola M., 1950
    Hospital / Lola Schaefer.
      p. cm. – (Who works here?)
    Includes bibliographical references and index.
    Summary: An introduction to the people who work at a hospital,
including doctors, nurses, physical therapists, admissions manager,
and speech pathologist.
    ISBN 1-57572-519-3 (library binding)
    1. Hospitals—Staff Juvenile literature.   [1. Hospitals.
2. Medical care. 3. Occupations.] 1. Title.   II. Series.
RA972.5.S285   2000
362.1'1—dc21   99-40761
                                                            CIP

Acknowledgments
All photographs by Phil Martin.

Special thanks to Cheryl Clark, Tammy Fisher, and the staff at DeKalb Memorial Hospital
in Auburn, Indiana, and to workers everywhere who take pride in what they do.

Every effort has been made to contact copyright holders of any material reproduced in this book.
Any omissions will be rectified in subsequent printings if notice is given to the publisher.

Some words are shown in bold, **like this.**
You can find out what they mean by looking in the glossary.

Contents

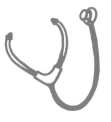

What Happens at a Hospital?

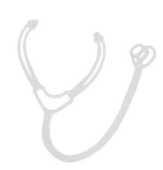

A hospital is a building where **medical** staff help sick or injured people. **Patients** go to a hospital for different reasons. Doctors **admit** patients who need surgery. Accident victims are brought to the hospital for medical **treatment.** Some patients are admitted for long-term care from the doctors and nurses.

Hospitals are open 24 hours a day, seven days a week. There is always a complete medical staff on duty. Everyone works together to give each patient the best health care.

This hospital is in Auburn, Indiana. This map shows where all of the people in this book are working. Many hospitals in the United States have the same departments.

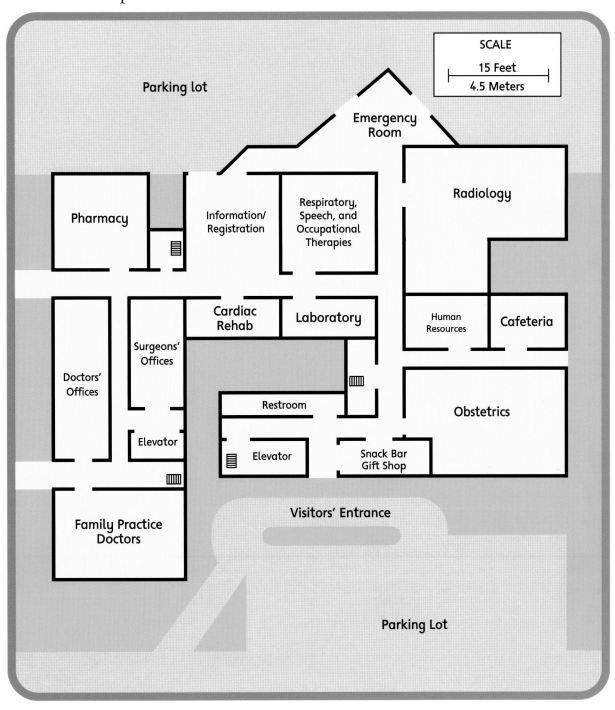

Assistant Administrator

Kelly is an assistant administrator. She uses a computer for many tasks, including typing reports.

An assistant administrator helps the hospital president **manage** the hospital. An important part of the assistant administrator's job is keeping the hospital safe for all workers, visitors, and **patients.** Other duties include checking that patients have healthy food and making sure that all cleaning work is done well.

An assistant administrator of a hospital needs a college **degree**. Many administrators study longer and earn a degree in Health Administration. Assistant administrators must be able to work with other hospital workers to solve the many problems that come up every day.

Kelly and the director of the lab talk about rules for ordering tests.

Admissions Manager

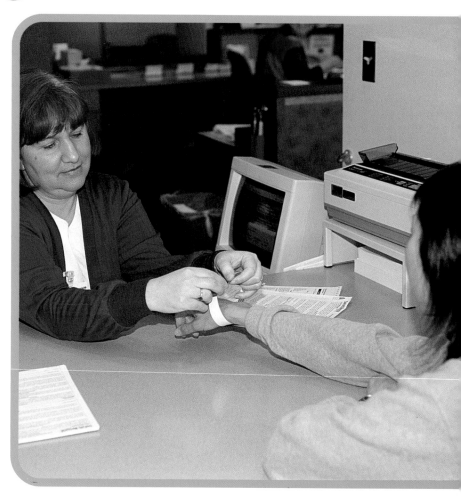

Barbara is an admissions manager. Here she puts an ID bracelet on a new patient.

An admissions manager **registers patients** as they enter the hospital. The admissions manager reads the doctor's orders and lists all needed **treatments.** Then, the admissions manager prepares an ID bracelet for the patient to wear during his or her visit.

An admissions manager trains for three months on the job. The admissions manager greets patients and helps them feel comfortable in the hospital. First, the admissions manager enters all patient information into the computer. Then **medical** records and **insurance** forms for each patient must be checked.

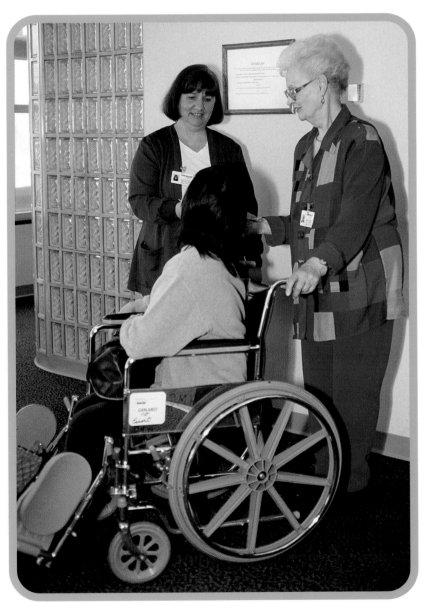

Here she asks that a patient be taken to a room.

Doctor

This is Doctor Khin. She listens carefully to her patient and takes notes.

Many doctors work in an office and in a hospital. **Patients** usually make **appointments** to see their doctors in their offices. If a patient needs further **medical** help, the doctor **admits** the person to the hospital. Doctors visit all of their hospital patients every day.

Doctors must go to school for many years. After going to college for four years, they must spend another four years in medical school. Afterward, they study with other doctors in a hospital for three years. Doctors need to know all about the body, medicines, and how to use the medical equipment correctly.

A patient asks the doctor when she can go home.

Nurse

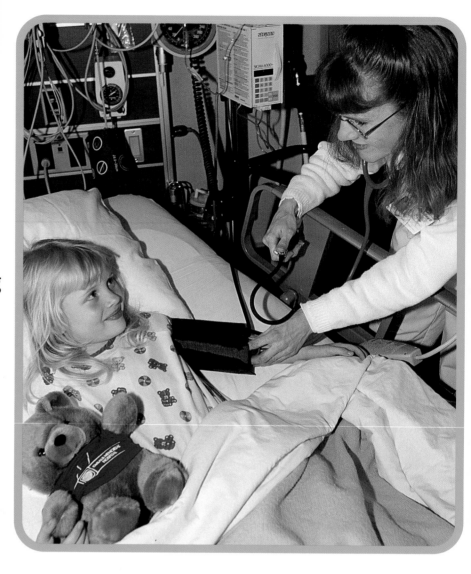

Deanna is a nurse in this hospital. Here she is measuring a girl's **blood pressure.**

A nurse in a hospital cares for the **patients** on a floor or in a special department of the hospital. Nurses give medicine to patients and **record** each dose on a chart for the doctors. The nurse takes the **vital signs** of the patients every few hours.

Deanna, like many nurses, went to college for three years. Nurses should enjoy helping people stay comfortable as they receive **medical treatment.** Before the patients leave the hospital, nurses teach them how to care for themselves at home.

Deanna often talks to a patient's family by telephone. She answers their questions and informs the family about the patient's health.

Lab Assistant

A lab assistant collects body fluids from **patients.** Each sample is tested. The results help doctors choose the correct **medical treatment** for the patient. A lab assistant always wears rubber gloves while working in the lab. This protects the lab assistant from germs and illnesses.

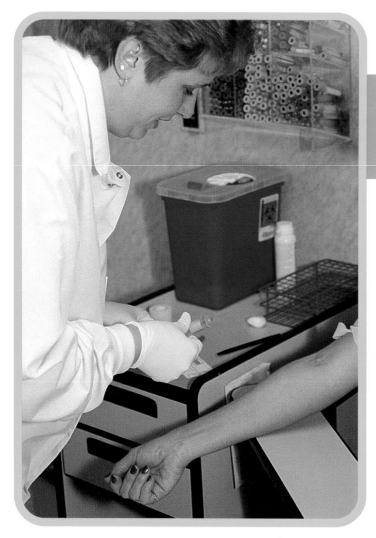

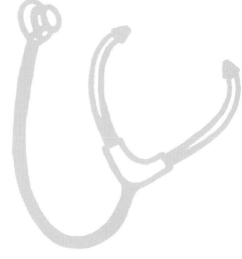

Candi is a lab assistant. She is preparing a patient for a blood test.

Candi prepares to separate blood cells
in this machine.

The lab assistant orders the tests from the doctor's
request. Then, the lab assistant collects the samples
from the patient, seals them, and labels each tube
with the patient's name and test. A lab assistant
works carefully to avoid mistakes. Test results must
be checked and rechecked.

Using Lab Equipment

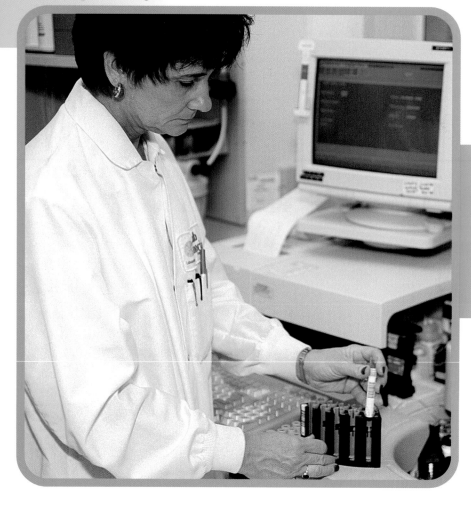

This machine can run several tests on one tube of blood.

Most lab equipment is controlled by computers. Each piece helps the staff run tests on different body fluid samples. All tubes are labeled with the **patient's** name and a bar code. A laser reads the bar code and then makes the machine run tests on the sample.

After each test, the computer prints out the results. Every computer in the lab is connected to the Lab Information System. This system quickly sends the test results to the doctor so the patient can get the correct **treatment.**

This machine tests the white and red blood cells.

Director of the Pharmacy

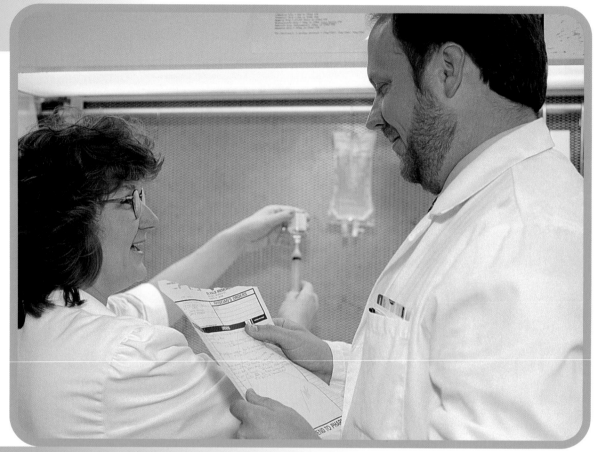

Norm is the director of the pharmacy. He helps
a new staff member with a patient's medicine.

The director of the **pharmacy** in a hospital oversees all
medicine that is prepared by the pharmacists for the
patients. He and his staff answer questions about the
different drugs for the doctors and nurses.

Like many pharmacists, Norm went to college for six years. Pharmacy students study the different types of drugs and how they affect the body. They also learn what drugs can be taken together. Pharmacists use math to decide the amount of medicine in each dose.

As director of the pharmacy, Norm must check the cost of each drug.

Director of Radiology

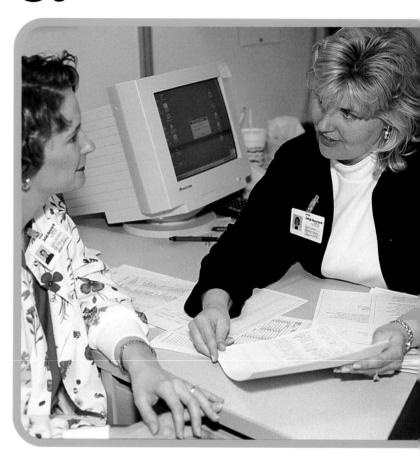

Paula is the director of radiology. Besides her other duties, Paula must also discuss the cost of X-rays with her staff.

The director of **radiology** is in charge of the X-ray equipment and the people who use it. The director hires the people who work in the department and schedules when they work. The director of radiology is always learning about new equipment and how it can help doctors provide better **medical** care for their **patients**.

The director of radiology must care about staff and patient safety. Everyone in the room during an X-ray needs to wear a **lead** apron. The X-ray beam can injure body cells through repeated **exposure.** Lead prevents X-rays from reaching the body.

Lead gloves protect the radiologist while she works with equipment.

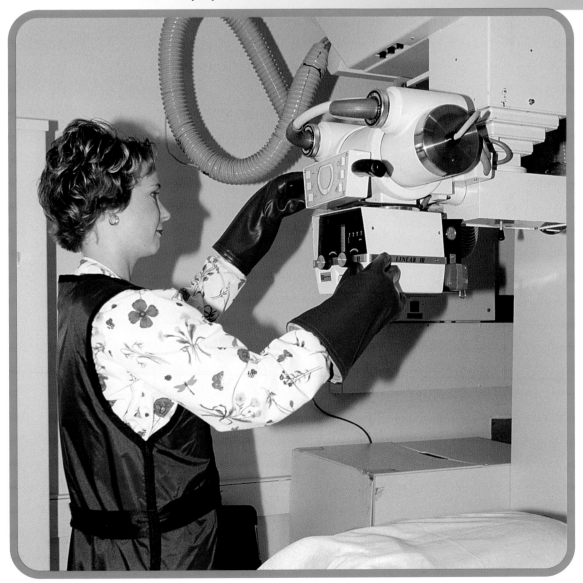

Using Radiology Equipment

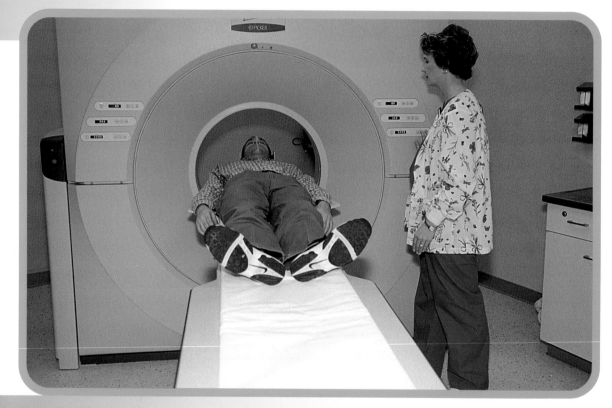

This radiologist uses a scanner to take pictures of the inside of this patient's head.

The **radiology** staff uses the most recent and **accurate** equipment. This helps them take pictures of the **organs** and **tissue** on the inside of a **patient's** body. These results help doctors choose **treatment** that will help the patients.

Some equipment, like this camera, is attached to a computer. As the camera takes pictures of the patient's organs, the radiology staff can view the pictures on the monitor. This machine is often used to study the heart, lungs, and bones.

Patients keep their clothes on while the camera takes pictures of their organs.

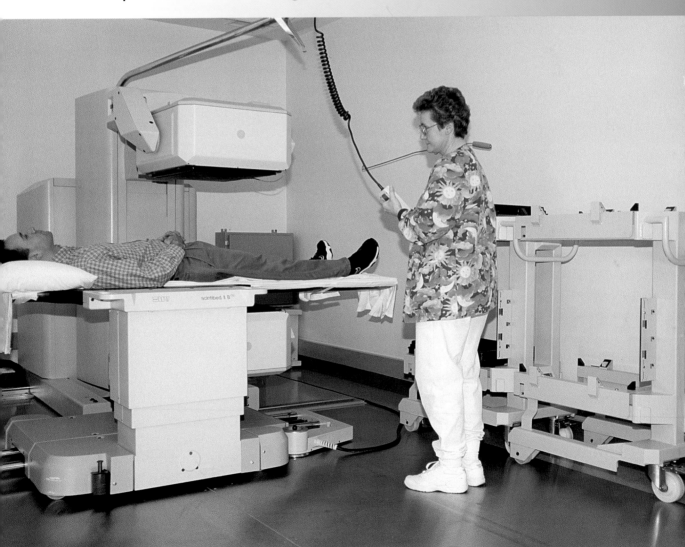

Physical Therapist

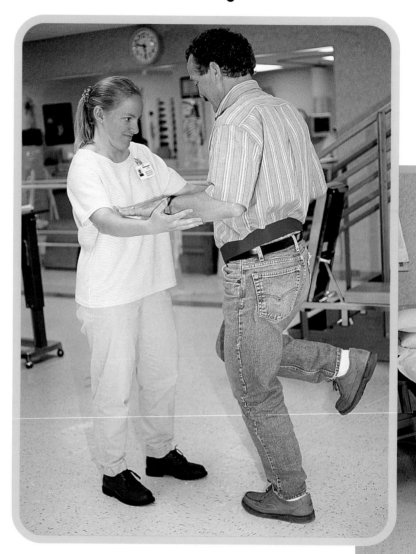

Amanda is a physical therapist. Here she helps a patient balance on one foot.

A physical therapist teaches **patients** the exercises needed to build strength in weak muscles. Sometimes a physical therapist helps a patient learn to walk with crutches or a walker. After surgery, the therapist teaches patients how to lift or move without harming their bodies.

Physical therapists usually go to college for six years. They must pass a test to become **licensed** by the state. All physical therapists continue their education at state and national meetings each year. At these meetings, they learn about new ways to help their patients.

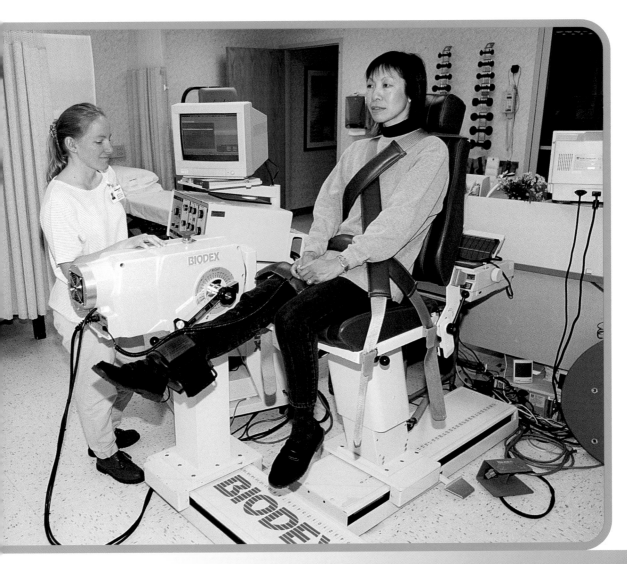

Amanda uses a machine to help a patient build strength in her knee.

Paramedic

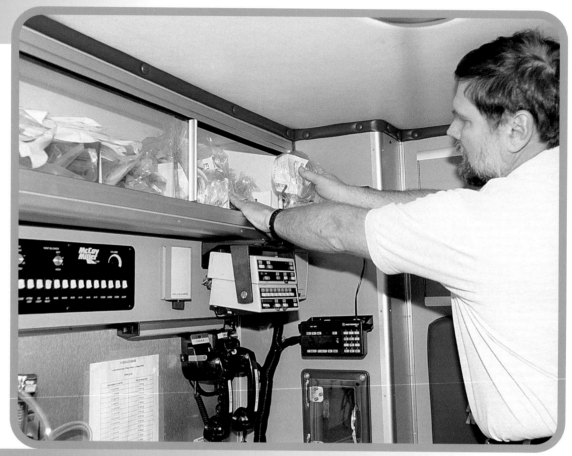

Randy is a paramedic. He must make sure that his ambulance has the correct supplies and is ready for all emergencies.

A paramedic brings people in need of immediate **medical** care to the hospital. A paramedic drives or rides in an ambulance with a partner. Sometimes, paramedics must give medicine or **treatment** to the **patient** on the way to the hospital.

Randy, like other paramedics, is **certified** by the state in which he lives. His training prepared him to offer emergency **medical** services to patients in his care. A paramedic stays in constant communication with the hospital staff when moving a patient. The hospital can tell the paramedics which treatment to use.

Randy and his partner have just delivered a patient to the hospital.

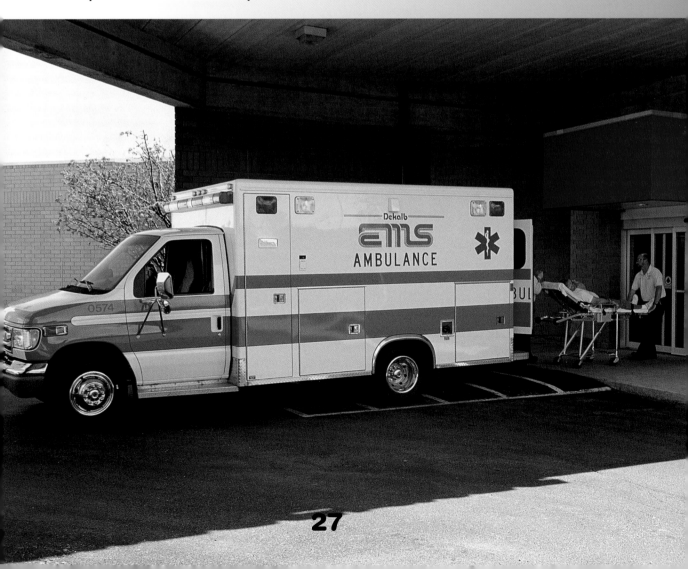

Speech Pathologist

A speech pathologist works with **patients** who have speech, swallowing, or hearing problems. The pathologist tests patients to decide the type and length of **treatment** that will meet their needs. Patients of all ages go to the hospital to meet with their speech pathologist.

Val, a speech pathologist, gives a young boy a hearing test.

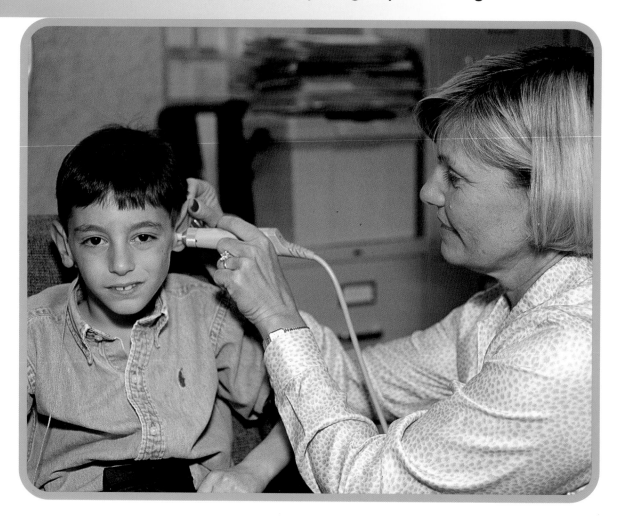

Val works with the computer to help a patient
use his voice.

Speech pathologists go to college for six or seven years.
During that time, they study how people move their
tongues to speak and swallow. They learn how people
hear. They learn how to test and measure skills. Many
speech pathologists learn sign language.

Glossary

accurate exact, correct

admit to allow someone to enter

appointment time agreed for a meeting

blood pressure force of blood pushing against blood vessels and arteries

certified able to do a job after passing a test

degree rank that a college gives a student who has finished his or her studies

exposure left without cover or protection

insurance money paid to a person for their medical bills when they are ill or injured

lead soft, gray metal that absorbs X-rays

licensed permitted by law to do something

manage to have control or charge of something

medical to do with doctors or medicine

organ part of an animal or human that has a special purpose

patient person who is treated by a doctor or dentist

pharmacy place where trained specialists prepare and sell medical drugs

radiology study of how X-rays can be used in medicine

record to write down

register to enter a name or information on an official list

tissue material that forms some part of a plant or animal, usually made up of cells

treatment way of trying to heal a sick or injured person

vital signs signs that show life, including breathing, pulse, and blood pressure

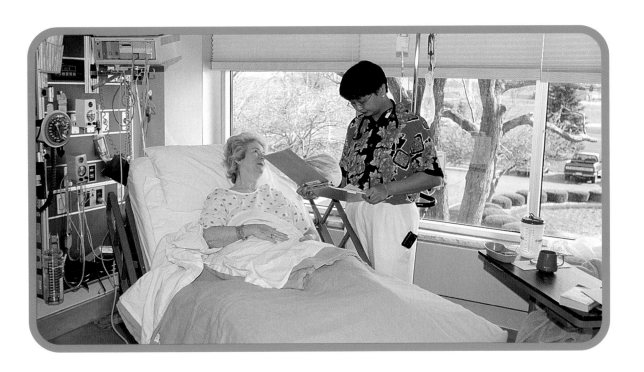

More Books to Read

Butler, Daphne. *First Look in the Hospital.* Milwaukee: Gareth Stevens Children's Books, 1991.

Dooley, Virginia. *Tubes in My Ears: My Trip to the Hospital.* Greenvale, N.Y.: Mondo, 1996.

Johnston, Marianne. *Let's Talk About When Someone You Love Is in the Hospital.* New York: PowerKids Press, 1997.

Miller, Marilyn. *Behind the Scenes at the Hospital.* Austin, Tex.: Raintree Steck-Vaughn, 1996.

Moses, Amy. *At the Hospital.* Chanhassen, Minn.: Child's World, 1997.

Index

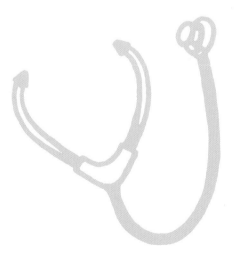

362,1
Sc

Schaefer
Hospital